GREAT TEAMS IN PRO FOOTBALL HISTORY

Joe Giglio

Raintree

Chicago, Illinois

Printed and bound in China by WKT Company Limited

10 09 08 07 06
10 9 8 7 6 5 4 3 2 1

Library of Congress Cataloging-in-Publication Data:

Giglio, Joe.
  Great teams in pro football history / Joe Giglio.
      p. cm. — (Great teams)
  Includes bibliographical references and index.
  ISBN 1-4109-1483-6 (hc) — ISBN 1-4109-1490-9 (pb)
  1. National Football League—History—20th century—Juvenile literature.
  2. Football teams—History—20th century—Juvenile literature. I. Title. II. Series.

GV955.5.N35G53 2006
796.332'64'0973—dc22

                                    2005011971
Acknowledgements
The publishers would like to thank the following for permission to reproduce photographs:
Corbis pp. 5 (Bettman), 6 (Bettman), 8 (Bettman), 9 (Bettman), 10 (Bettman), 11 (Bettman), 12 (Bettman), 16 (Bettman), 23 (Bettman), 24 (S. Carmona), 44 (NewSport/Tim Tadder), 28 (Reuters/Gary Hershorn); Empics pp. 4 (AP/Brett Coomer), 15 (AP), 19 (AP), 25 (AP/Rusty Kennedy), 30 (AP/Tim Sharp), 38 (AP/L. G. Patterson), 42 (AP/Mike J. Terrill), 40 (AP/Winslow Townson); Getty Images pp. 14 (Focus on Sport), 20 (Diamond Images); Reuters pp. 26 (Gary Hershorn), 32 (Mike Blake), 33 (Mike Segar), 41 (Mike Segar); Wire Image pp. 17 (NFL Photos/Vernon Biever), 22 (Al Messerschmidt); Zuma Press pp. 31 (The Sporting News/Rich Pilling), 35 (The Sporting News/Albert Dickson), 39 (The Sporting News/Bob Leverone), 36 (The Sporting News/Dilip Vishwanat).

Cover image of Emmitt Smith reproduced with permission of Getty Images.

Every effort has been made to contact the copyright holders of any material reproduced in this book. Any omissions will be rectified in subsequent printings if notice is given to the publishers.

The paper used to print this book comes from sustainable resources.

Disclaimer: This book is not authorized or approved by any football team or league.

Contents

Any words appearing in the text in bold, **like this**, are explained in the glossary.

Welcome to the Game

An estimated 134 million people in the United States watched the **Super Bowl** on television in 2004. During that year more than 17 million people attended **National Football League (NFL)** games! With that amount of fans, can you believe that at one time professional football was not very popular? Before football became what it is today, baseball was the most popular sport in the country and had the most famous players. Players such as Babe Ruth and **franchises** such as the New York Yankees amazed fans. Football, on the other hand, was thought of as a dangerous sport. But gradually, football has become America's favorite sport. It now beats baseball, basketball, and any other sport in game attendance and television ratings.

The history of professional football goes way back. Professional football got its start in Pennsylvania, with club and traveling teams competing in leagues.

The NFL officially formed in 1922. The league originally had fourteen teams from previously existing, but unsuccessful, leagues. It took almost 40 years for football to make its mark on the public. Not even **dominant** teams such as the 1940 Chicago Bears, who won the NFL Championship game 73–0, could boost the game's popularity.

This is an overhead view of Super Bowl XXXVIII at Houston's Reliant Stadium.

The television boom in the United States in the 1950s began to change all that. With a fast pace and frequent breaks that were very convenient for commercials, football was made for television. American audiences tuned into the 1958 NFL championship game between the Baltimore Colts and the New York Giants. Often referred to as "The Greatest Game Ever Played," more than 50 million people watched the Colts beat the Giants in **overtime**.

The Baltimore Colts win their first league championship 23–17 against the New York Giants on December 28, 1958.

After the 1966 season, the NFL and the American Football League (AFL), a rival professional football league, competed in a made-for-television championship. The winning teams from these two leagues met in a championship title game that would later become known as the Super Bowl. Soon, with the excitement brought by the Super Bowl, every large city in the United States wanted a professional football team. Today, the NFL has 32 teams and is divided into 2 **conferences**, the National Football Conference (NFC) and the American Football Conference (AFC). These conferences are further divided into regional divisions. Some of these divisions have intense rivalries, such as the Green Bay Packers and the Chicago Bears. Each season, the six best teams from each conference qualify for the playoffs and the winners get to go to the Super Bowl.

This book looks at ten of the greatest teams in pro football history. Good teams have earned their place in history with a solid offense, a tough defense, a committed coach, or talented players. A truly great team, however, has a combination of all of these. The best players and teams make and break records, set good examples for young fans, and are generally fun to watch. After you read this book, you can decide which team in pro football you think is the greatest in history.

1950 Cleveland Browns

The Cleveland Browns' long tradition of professional football dates back to 1946. Their beginning was definitely a strong one. From 1946 to 1949, the Cleveland Browns won the newly formed All-America Football Conference (AAFC) championship each year. When the Browns became part of the NFL in 1950, the team wasn't expected to repeat their championship success.

Some members of the 1950 Cleveland Browns line up for a team photo.

However, Coach Paul Brown had other ideas. He wasn't going to let the team give up. It didn't take long for the Browns to prove that they could win it all. The Browns were led by **Pro Football Hall of Fame quarterback** Otto Graham, league **rushing** leader Marion Motley, and end Dante Lavelli on offense. Hall-of-Famers Bill Willis and Len Ford were on defense.

In their NFL debut in 1950, the Browns went up against the Philadelphia Eagles, the NFL champion from 1949. The champion versus champion game proved to be an easy win for the Browns. They beat the Eagles 35–10. The Browns beat the Eagles again in the twelfth week of the season, with a score of 13–7.

The Browns went on to finish the regular season with a 10–2 record. They were tied with the New York Giants for first place. The Giants had given the Browns their only two losses that season. The Giants beat the Browns 6–0 in Cleveland and later in the season 17–13 in New York. The Giants were looking for a third win in the playoffs. However, it was the determined Browns who won the third game 8–3 and earned a trip to the NFL championship game.

HISTORY BOX

Back in the NFL

The Cleveland Browns have a long history with many great players. This is why the team shocked Cleveland fans and football fans everywhere when it left Cleveland for three seasons, from 1996 to 1998. Browns' owner Art Modell moved the team to Baltimore after an argument with city leaders about building a new stadium. When the Browns moved, they became the Baltimore Ravens. This left Cleveland without an NFL team for three seasons. Thankfully, a football team was reorganized in Cleveland in 1999 with new ownership, a new roster and coaching staff, and a new downtown stadium. Unfortunately, in the old team's absence, Cleveland fans missed out on a title. The Baltimore Ravens, made up of former Browns players, won the Super Bowl in 2000.

1950 Cleveland Browns

In the 1950 NFL championship game, the Browns faced the Los Angeles Rams. The Rams were a franchise that had actually played in Cleveland from 1937 to 1945. The Browns were up against another great team and the game was tough. The Browns won the game 30–28 for their fifth championship in their fifth year of being a team! The Browns, led by Coach Paul Brown, had an amazing start in the NFL. In their first six years in the NFL they reached the NFL championship six times. They won the title again in 1954 and 1955.

Browns' quarterback Otto Graham carries the ball to win against the Los Angeles Rams in the 1950 NFL championship game.

1950 Record

Won	Lost	NFL Divisional Championship	NFL Championship Game
12	2	Beat New York Giants 8–3	Beat Los Angeles Rams 30–28

Games played

Week	Vs	Result	Score
1	at Philadelphia Eagles	W	35–10
2	at Baltimore Colts	W	31–0
3	New York Giants	L	0–6
4	at Pittsburgh Steelers	W	30–17
5	Chicago Cardinals	W	34–24
6	at New York Giants	L	13–17
7	Pittsburgh Steelers	W	45–7
8	at Chicago Cardinals	W	10–7
9	San Francisco 49ers	W	34–14
10	Washington Redskins	W	20–14
11	BYE WEEK		
12	Philadelphia Eagles	W	13–7
13	at Washington Redskins	W	45–21

W=Won, L=Lost

Paul Brown (1908–1991)

Paul Brown had a huge influence on the game of football. He helped create two teams currently in the NFL—the Cleveland Browns and the Cincinnati Bengals. In 1945, Arthur McBride, the owner of an AAFC team coming to Cleveland, held a contest in the newspapers to name the team. The overwhelming response from readers favored the name the Browns, after the very popular Paul Brown who was to be the team's coach. In seventeen seasons, Brown won four AAFC titles and three NFL titles. He had just one losing season in his career as founder, owner, and coach of the Browns. In 1968, Brown also helped create the Bengals, an expansion team. He coached the Bengals until 1975 and acted as the team's owner until his death in 1991. Brown's family still owns the team. The Bengals' stadium that opened in 2000 is called the Paul Brown Stadium.

1950 Cleveland Browns

Pro Bowlers:

Tony Adamle	(RB)	Marion Motley	(RB)
Otto Graham	(QB)	Mac Speedie	(WR)
Weldon Humble	(OL)	Bill Willis	(DL)

Head coach: Paul Brown

RB=Running Back, QB=Quarterback, OL=Offensive Lineman, WR=Wide Receiver, DL=Defensive Lineman

1962 Green Bay Packers

The Green Bay Packers won five NFL championships from 1961 to 1967. No other team had done this before and no team has done it since. With legendary coach Vince Lombardi and ten Hall-of-Fame players, the Packers of the 1960s are considered one of football's mightiest teams. Perhaps their best season came in 1962. With one title already in hand, the Packers' best players still had their best year in front of them. These players were: Jim Taylor, offensive **lineman** Forrest Gregg, quarterback Bart Starr, **linebacker** Ray Nitschke, **cornerback** Herb Adderley, **defensive end** Willie Davis, **center** Jim Ringo, **halfback** Paul Hornung, **safety** Willie Wood, and **defensive tackle** Henry Jordan.

Green Bay Packer Paul Hornung scores against the St. Louis Cardinals. The Packers won the game 17–0.

In 1962, the Packers were determined to succeed and they pulled together as a team. During their 14-game regular-season schedule, the Packers won 13 times and lost just once in a 26–14 defeat against the Detroit Lions. Despite this loss, the Packers were unstoppable. They outscored their opponents 415 to 148. They scored the most points in the league and allowed their opponents the fewest points. They had three **shutouts**. Two of these games had scores of 49–0. Vince Lombardi, who turned the Packers from a losing franchise into the greatest team of the **decade**, relied mostly on a tough running game instead of a passing game. With Taylor and Hornung, the Packers were able to gain a huge number of **yards**. Taylor, a **fullback**, had a great year in 1962. He gained 1,474 yards and set a NFL record with 19 touchdowns.

Packers' player Jim Taylor avoids being tackled in a game against the Philadelphia Eagles.

Another important player was Hall-of-Fame quarterback Bart Starr, who threw for a career-best 2,438 yards in 1962 with 12 touchdowns. Starr had good **wide receivers** in Max McGee and Boyd Dowler, who each caught 49 passes. **Tight end** Ron Kramer caught 37 passes, including a team-best 7 receiving touchdowns.

1962 Green Bay Packers

After completing the regular season 13–1, the Packers reached the NFL championship game. A year earlier in Green Bay, the Packers embarrassed the New York Giants with a 37–0 win to earn the title. The 1962 championship title game was played in New York at Yankee Stadium. **Running back** Jim Taylor of the Packers stood in the way of the Giants' revenge! Fighting both the cold weather and the Giants' defense, Taylor carried the ball 31 times for 85 yards and Green Bay's only touchdown in a 16–7 victory. During the game, Taylor suffered an elbow cut that took seven stitches to close and he also badly cut his tongue. By the end, he could barely talk, but like the rest of the 1962 Green Bay Packers, Taylor was a champion!

Vince Lombardi (1913–1970)

The season before Vince Lombardi became the head coach of the Green Bay Packers, the team won exactly one game. The Green Bay championship glory years of Earl "Curly" Lambeau were long gone by the time 45-year-old Lombardi joined the Packers. Lombardi relied on the running game, a strong offensive line, and team motivation. No coach got more out of his players than Lombardi, who once said, "Winning is not everything, but wanting to win is." But Lombardi did win. He went 98–30–4 (wins–losses–ties) overall in 9 seasons with the Green Bay Packers. Almost 35 years after he retired, ESPN named Lombardi "Coach of the Century." When the NFL and AFL decided to play the first Super Bowl in 1966, Lombardi's Packers won the game 35–10 over the Kansas City Chiefs. The Packers won again the following year 33–14 over the Oakland Raiders. To this day, the Super Bowl winner is presented with the Vince Lombardi Trophy, in honor of the great coach.

Vince Lombardi is considered by many to be one of the greatest coaches in football history.

HISTORY BOX

Return to Titletown

When the Packers were winning NFL titles, the city of Green Bay's nickname of "Titletown, USA" made sense. But what did they call the Wisconsin town from 1969 to 1996? The Packers, who are actually owned by the city's residents instead of just one owner, went without a title for all of those years. The Packers won Super Bowls I and II, but had to wait until Super Bowl XXXI to claim another title. The Packers struggled up until that point. It wasn't until the mid-1990s that coach Mike Holmgren and quarterback Brett Favre rebuilt the Packers into an NFL power. After the 1996 season, they beat the New England Patriots 35–21 to win Super Bowl XXXI.

1962 Green Bay Packers

Pro Bowlers:

Bill Forester	(LB)
Forrest Gregg	(OL)
Jerry Kramer	(OL)
Ron Kramer	(TE)
Tom Moore	(RB)
Jim Ringo	(OL)
Bart Starr	(QB)
Jim Taylor	(RB)
Willie Wood	(DB)

Head coach: Vince Lombardi

LB=Linebacker, TE=Tight End, DB=Defensive Back

1962 Record

Won	Lost	NFL Championship Game
14	1	Beat New York Giants 16–7

Games played

Week	Vs	Result	Score
1	Minnesota Vikings	W	34–7
2	St. Louis Cardinals	W	17–0
3	Chicago Bears	W	49–0
4	Detroit Lions	W	9–7
5	at Minnesota Vikings	W	48–21
6	San Francisco 49ers	W	31–13
7	at Baltimore Colts	W	17–6
8	at Chicago Bears	W	38–7
9	at Philadelphia Eagles	W	49–0
10	Baltimore Colts	W	17–13
11	at Detroit Lions	L	14–26
12	Los Angeles Rams	W	41–10
13	at San Francisco 49ers	W	31–21
14	at Los Angeles Rams	W	20–17

1972 Miami Dolphins

The 1972 Miami Dolphins were a unique team. They won all of the seventeen games that they played in the 1972 season. In the NFL's history, the Dolphins are the only team that has finished both the regular season and the playoffs without a loss.

The Dolphins had Hall-of-Fame talent as well as a great coach, Don Shula. The Dolphins were known for their impressive running attack led by Larry Csonka, Jim Kiick, and Mercury Morris. Nick Buoniconti led the Dolphins' defense, which became known as the "No-Name Defense" because the team's offense got more publicity.

Although the Dolphins finished the season undefeated, they had faced many challenges during the year. In their third game of the season, the Dolphins trailed the Minnesota Vikings 14–6 before making a fourth-quarter comeback for a 16–14 win. During their fifth game, starting quarterback Bob Griese broke his right leg. Earl Morrall, a 38-year-old veteran, filled in for the injured Griese. The Dolphins won the game and continued to stay on top under Morrall's strong playing. In the tenth game of the season, the Dolphins again found themselves down in the fourth quarter. Trailing 24–20 to the New York Jets, Miami needed all 107 rushing yards from Morris to come back and win 28–24.

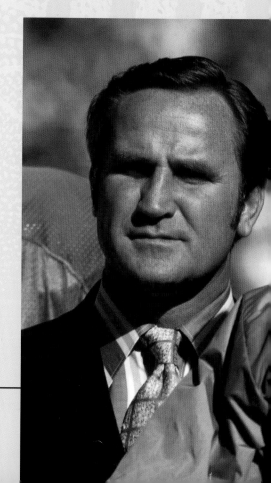

The playoffs provided yet another test for the Dolphins. They fell behind the Cleveland Browns 14–13 in the fourth quarter. The Dolphins couldn't let their incredible season end early. Jim Kiick finished off an 80-yard drive with an 8-yard touchdown run to give Miami the lead for good. The Dolphins moved onto the AFC championship game. Eleven weeks after breaking his leg, Griese returned to help the Dolphins beat the Pittsburgh Steelers in Pittsburgh in the AFC championship game.

Miami Dolphins' coach Don Shula holds the record for most wins in pro football history.

Despite being 16–0, the Dolphins went into Super Bowl VII as an **underdog** to the Washington Redskins. The Redskins had won the NFC after an 11–3 regular season and had beaten the Dallas Cowboys and Green Bay Packers in the playoffs. Washington didn't have a chance, though, against the Dolphins' "No-Name Defense" in the Super Bowl.

1972 Miami Dolphins

Pro Bowlers:

Dick Anderson	(DB)	Mercury Morris	(RB)
Nick Buoniconti	(LB)	Jake Scott	(DB)
Larry Csonka	(RB)	Bill Stanfill	(DL)
Norm Evans	(OL)	Paul Warfield	(WR)
Larry Little	(OL)		

Head coach: Don Shula

1972 Record

Won	Lost	AFC Divisional Playoff
17	0	Beat Cleveland Browns 20–14

AFC Championship Game	Super Bowl
Beat Pittsburgh Steelers 21–17	Beat Washington Redskins 14–7

Games played

Week	Vs	Result	Score
1	at Kansas City Chiefs	W	20–10
2	Houston Oilers	W	34–13
3	at Minnesota Vikings	W	16–14
4	at New York Jets	W	27–17
5	San Diego Chargers	W	24–10
6	Buffalo Bills	W	24–23
7	at Baltimore Colts	W	23–0
8	at Buffalo Bills	W	30–16
9	New England Patriots	W	52–0
10	New York Jets	W	28–24
11	St. Louis Cardinals	W	31–10
12	at New England Patriots	W	37–21
13	at New York Giants	W	23–13
14	Baltimore Colts	W	16–0

1975 Pittsburgh Steelers

The NFL really started to become popular in the 1970s. During this time, there were great teams and bad teams, but not many teams that fell in the middle. The 1975 Pittsburgh Steelers were one of the great teams. They won four Super Bowl titles in a six-year span from 1974 to 1979. When the NFL announced its 75th Anniversary Team in 1994, 5 players from these great Steeler teams made the list: center Mike Webster, linebacker Jack Ham, linebacker Jack Lambert, cornerback Mel Blount, and defensive end Joe Greene. Four of these players created the backbone of the Steelers' defense, which was nicknamed "The Steel Curtain." An amazing ten of the eleven defensive starters in 1975 were **Pro Bowl** players at one point in their careers. At the beginning of the 1970s, the Pittsburgh Steelers weren't a great team at all. It was coach Chuck Knoll who turned the team around. He **drafted** eight players who went on to finish their careers in the Pro Football Hall of Fame. One of these players was quarterback Terry Bradshaw. Drafted in the first round out of Louisiana Tech in 1970, Bradshaw was put in the starting lineup soon afterwards.

Pittsburgh Steelers players pose for photos in 1975.

At first he was unpopular and **inconsistent** and was booed by fans. He threw 46 interceptions in his first 2 seasons, and the Steelers won just 11 games in the 1971 and 1972 seasons combined. However, as Bradshaw gained experience, and Knoll filled the team with other talented players, the fortunes of both the quarterback and the team began to change. By 1974 the Steelers were Super Bowl champions and in 1975 they had their best season. The Steelers repeated as champions, and Bradshaw earned his first Pro Bowl appearance that year. He threw for 2,055 yards and 18 touchdowns with just 9 interceptions.

Steelers' linebackers Jack Ham and Andy Russell tackle an opponent.

1975 Record

Won	Lost
15	2

AFC Divisional Playoff
Beat Baltimore Colts 28–10

AFC Championship Game
Beat Oakland Raiders 16–10

Super Bowl
Beat Dallas Cowboys 21–17

Games played

Week	Vs	Result	Score
1	at San Diego Chargers	W	37–0
2	Buffalo Bills	L	21–30
3	at Cleveland Browns	W	42–6
4	Denver Broncos	W	20–9
5	Chicago Bears	W	34–3
6	at Green Bay Packers	W	16–13
7	at Cincinnati Bengals	W	30–24
8	Houston Oilers	W	24–17
9	Kansas City Chiefs	W	28–3
10	at Houston Oilers	W	32–9
11	at New York Jets	W	20–7
12	Cleveland Browns	W	31–17
13	Cincinnati Bengals	W	35–14
14	at Los Angeles Rams	L	3–10

1975 Pittsburgh Steelers

After losing to the Buffalo Bills in the second week of the season, the Steelers had eleven straight wins. They lost the last game of the regular season to finish with a record of 12–2. Terry Bradshaw had plenty of help on offense. Running back Franco Harris and **receiver** Lynn Swann both made the Pro Bowl. Harris led the team and ranked second in the NFL with 1,246 rushing yards. Swann caught 49 passes for 781 yards with 11 touchdowns. Back then these were huge numbers. The Steelers, like most of football's truly great teams, relied on good defense and a running game to win championships.

In the playoffs, the Steelers hoped to repeat their Super Bowl title from the previous season. The Steelers were able to beat the Baltimore Colts 28–10 in the divisional playoff and advanced to the AFC championship game to play their rival, the Oakland Raiders. They survived against the Raiders with a 16–10 win and advanced on to the Super Bowl.

1975 Pittsburgh Steelers

Pro Bowlers:

Mel Blount (DB)	Franco Harris (RB)
Terry Bradshaw (QB)	Jack Lambert (LB)
Glen Edwards (DB)	Andy Russell (LB)
Joe Greene (DL)	Lynn Swann (WR)
L.C. Greenwood (DL)	Mike Wagner (DB)
Jack Ham (LB)	

Head coach: Chuck Knoll

The Steelers had to get by the Dallas Cowboys in Super Bowl X. The Cowboys went 10–4 during the regular season with quarterback Roger Staubach. The Steelers would have to try something different to beat the determined team. Instead of focusing on running the ball, Terry Bradshaw threw the ball to Lynn Swann for a 64-yard touchdown pass. Swann ended the game with 4 catches for a then Super Bowl record of 161 yards. The Steelers defeated the Dallas Cowboys 21–17 and earned another championship title.

Terry Bradshaw (1948–   )

Quarterback Terry Bradshaw was not popular when he first started playing professional football. As the Steelers improved, so did Bradshaw. He and Joe Montana are the only quarterbacks who can claim four Super Bowl titles. Bradshaw, now a successful television commentator, even won the Super Bowl MVP twice. He retired in 1983. Bradshaw was cheered all the way to the Pro Football Hall of Fame in 1989 with 27,989 career passing yards and 212 touchdowns.

Pittsburgh's Lynn Swann dives to catch a pass from quarterback Terry Bradshaw in Super Bowl X against the Dallas Cowboys.

The Steelers won two more Super Bowls before the decade ended. They beat the Cowboys in a rematch after the 1978 season and the Rams after the 1979 season to become the first NFL team with four Super Bowl wins.

1985 Chicago Bears

Many consider the 1985 Chicago Bears to be one of the best teams to play the game of football. With linebacker Mike Singletary in the middle leading the defense and with a Pro Bowl player at nearly every position, the Bears were a powerful force. The Bears played nineteen games that season. They didn't allow the other team to score a single point in four of the games, and in fourteen games they only allowed their opponents to score ten points or less.

The Chicago Bears' defense huddles before a play in a game against the New York Jets on December 14, 1985.

1985 Chicago Bears

Pro Bowlers:

Jim Covert	(OL)	Jim McMahon	(QB)
Richard Dent	(DL)	Walter Payton	(RB)
Dave Duerson	(DB)	Mike Singletary	(LB)
Dan Hampton	(DL)	Otis Wilson	(LB)
Jay Hilgenberg	(OL)		

Head coach: Mike Ditka

1985 Record

Won	Lost	NFC Divisional Playoff
18	1	Beat New York Giants 21–0

NFC Championship Game
Beat Los Angeles Rams 24–0

Super Bowl
Beat New England Patriots 46–10

Games played

Week	Vs	Result	Score
1	Tampa Bay Buccaneers	W	38–28
2	New England Patriots	W	20–7
3	at Minnesota Vikings	W	33–24
4	Washington Redskins	W	45–10
5	at Tampa Bay Buccaneers	W	27–19
6	at San Francisco 49ers	W	26–10
7	Green Bay Packers	W	23–7
8	Minnesota Vikings	W	27–9
9	at Green Bay Packers	W	16–10
10	Detroit Lions	W	24–3
11	at Dallas Cowboys	W	44–0
12	Atlanta Falcons	W	36–0
13	at Miami Dolphins	L	24–38
14	Indianapolis Colts	W	17–10
15	at New York Jets	W	19–6
16	at Detroit Lions	W	37–17

The Bears scored the most points in the league. They dominated opponents with defensive **blitzes** that confused quarterbacks. The team had the perfect combination of size, speed, and strength on the defensive line. Defensive ends Dan Hampton and Richard Dent, linebacker Otis Wilson, and safety Dave Duerson led the Bears' strong defense along with Singletary. All of these players made the Pro Bowl in 1985 except for Dent—who led the NFL in sacks with seventeen and was awarded a much bigger honor by the end of the season.

For the first three months of the season, the 1985 Bears were unmatched by other teams. In November, they won 3 straight games by a combined score of 104–3. The Bears were 12–0 by the time December came. This soon changed. On a Monday night game in Miami, Florida, the Miami Dolphins beat the Bears. It was Chicago's only loss for the entire season. The Bears won their final 3 games and entered the playoffs with a 15–1 record.

The Bears improved even more in the playoffs. The team shutout the New York Giants in the divisional round by a score of 21–0. The Bears continued their shutout streak in a snowy NFC championship game with a 24–0 win over the Los Angeles Rams. In two playoff games, both of the opposing teams had no points!

All season long, the Bears won over fans in Chicago and around the country with an interesting mix of personalities. Coach Mike Ditka, or "Iron Mike," had been a Hall-of-Fame tight end for the Bears and had played for the legendary coach, George Halas. Mike Singletary, the defensive leader, was a very serious player. Running back Walter Payton was very graceful on the field. Then there were the crazy personalities of rookie William "Refrigerator" Perry, a gigantic defensive tackle turned part-time running back, and the "Punky" quarterback, Jim McMahon. This mixture of coach and players really appealed to football fans. Even before the Super Bowl, the Bears recorded a song, "The Super Bowl Shuffle," which was played on radio stations in January of 1986. "We're so bad, we know we're good," the Bears bragged in their song.

Bears' quarterback Jim McMahon looks to pass in Super Bowl XX.

HISTORY BOX

"The Super Bowl Shuffle"

While the Bears were winning on the field, they were becoming quite popular off it as well. The Bears were actually famous on the music charts. Before the Super Bowl, the Bears, including quarterback Jim McMahon, running back Walter Payton, and rookie defensive tackle William Perry recorded a song, "The Super Bowl Shuffle." It dominated radio stations in January of 1986.

The Bears certainly proved they were good in Super Bowl XX, in New Orleans. The Bears defeated the New England Patriots 46–10. Dent earned the game's **Most Valuable Player (MVP)** for leading a defense that allowed the Patriots to cross the 50-yard line only twice all game. The game scored huge with television viewers. The broadcast attracted more than 127 million viewers and a 70 share. That means that 70 percent of the people in the United States were watching the Bears win the Super Bowl! Perry, all 350 pounds of him, even scored a short touchdown to seal the victory and the unforgettable 1985 season.

Walter Payton (1954–1999)

While the Bears' defense gets most of the attention for the Bears' historic 1985 season, the team's offense had its share of stars. None were bigger than Walter Payton. "Sweetness," as Payton was called, gained 1,551 yards in 1985 to lead the NFL in rushing and to help the Bears average an impressive 28.5 points. Payton was the perfect complement to the Bears' defense. The defense would keep the opponents out of the **end zone**, and Payton would run the clock down, turning second-half leads into sure victories. When he retired in 1987, Payton finished as the NFL career leading rusher with 16,726 yards. He scored 125 touchdowns during his career. Payton reached 1,000 yards rushing in a season a record 10 times. He was inducted into the Pro Football Hall of Fame in 1993. Sadly, in 1999 Payton died of cancer.

1989 San Francisco 49ers

The San Francisco 49ers, also known simply as the Niners, have won a record five Super Bowl titles. A lot of the team's success can be credited to its coaches. Coach Bill Walsh led the 49ers for many years. Walsh really built up the franchise, with players such as quarterback Joe Montana and receiver Jerry Rice. Walsh retired after the 1988 season and turned the Niners over to a defensive coach, George Seifert. The 1989 49ers team had so much player talent that they went 14–2 under first-year coach, Siefert.

Players on the 1989 49ers team wave to the camera.

Joe Montana (1956–   )

Joe Montana was a genius quarterback. He was the best player in the game in the 1980s. Montana won four Super Bowls and three Super Bowl MVP awards with the Niners from 1982 to 1989. He ended his career after two seasons with the Kansas City Chiefs in 1994 and was inducted into the Pro Football Hall of Fame six years later.

The 49ers had won 3 Super Bowl titles under Bill Walsh from 1982 to 1988. One of the best players on the team, a player that had been recruited by Walsh, was quarterback Joe Montana. By 1989, Montana had reached superstar status. So just how good was Joe Montana in 1989? He completed more than 70 percent of his passes (271–386) for 3,521 yards and 28 touchdowns. That's an amazing feat! He also had a lot of talent around him that could not be matched, such as wide receiver Jerry Rice. Rice caught 82 passes in 1989 for more than 1,400 yards and 17 touchdowns. Running back Roger Craig ran for more than 1,000 yards. The Niners' Tom Rathman made 73 catches that season as the team's fullback.

1989 San Francisco 49ers

The 49ers led the NFL in scoring offense and ranked third in scoring defense, led by defensive end Charles Haley and Hall-of-Fame safety Ronnie Lott. The true measure of greatness for this 1989 San Francisco team came after their 14–2 regular season. In the playoffs, the Niners outscored three opponents 126 to 26 and won by an average of 36 points per game. They beat the Minnesota Vikings 41–13 in the divisional round and the Los Angeles Rams 30–3 in the NFC championship game.

Jerry Rice signals victory after scoring his touchdown in Super Bowl XXIII.

HISTORY BOX

The "West Coast Offense"

Created by former San Francisco coach Bill Walsh and his many former assistant coaches, the "West Coast Offense" was an offense that relied on short passes and lots of movement. The key to the offense is a quarterback who can throw well and receivers who can turn short passes into long gains. The Niners produced two of the most talented quarterbacks in NFL history—Joe Montana and Steve Young. The team's receivers were amazing, too—particularly Jerry Rice, who holds the NFL records for catches, touchdowns, and receiving yards. In the late 1990s, the Green Bay Packers used the same kind of offense to win the Super Bowl under quarterback Brett Favre. The Philadelphia Eagles, Oakland Raiders, and Tampa Bay Buccaneers have all advanced to the Super Bowl with the help of Walsh's offense.

The Niners then went on to set a Super Bowl record for points in a 55–10 defeat of the Denver Broncos. In the Super Bowl, Montana played an amazing game. He completed 22 of 29 passes for 297 yards and had a record 5 touchdowns, including 3 to Rice. Montana won his third Super Bowl MVP award.

1989 San Francisco 49ers

Pro Bowlers:

Roger Craig	(RB)	Joe Montana	(QB)
Ronnie Lott	(DB)	Jerry Rice	(WR)
Guy McIntyre	(OL)	John Taylor	(WR)

Head coach: George Seifert

1989 Record

Won	Lost	**NFC Divisional Playoff**
17	2	Beat Minnesota Vikings 41–13

NFC Championship Game
Beat Los Angeles Rams 30–3

Super Bowl
Beat Denver Broncos 55–10

Games played

Week	Vs	Result	Score
1	at Indianapolis Colts	W	30–24
2	at Tampa Bay Buccaneers	W	20–16
3	at Philadelphia Eagles	W	38–28
4	Los Angeles Rams	L	12–13
5	at New Orleans Saints	W	24–20
6	at Dallas Cowboys	W	31–14
7	New England Patriots	W	37–20
8	at New York Jets	W	23–10
9	New Orleans Saints	W	31–13
10	Atlanta Falcons	W	45–3
11	Green Bay Packers	L	17–21
12	New York Giants	W	34–24
13	at Atlanta Falcons	W	23–10
14	at Los Angeles Rams	W	30–27
15	Buffalo Bills	W	21–10
16	Chicago Bears	W	26–0

1992 Dallas Cowboys

After winning a national championship in college football, Jimmy Johnson took over as the Dallas Cowboys' coach in 1989. Right away, he was determined to win a Super Bowl championship. In Johnson's first season, the Cowboys won one game and lost fifteen. But Johnson and owner Jerry Jones planned to build the Cowboys with speed and talent. With one trade, the Cowboys succeeded in both of these things. Dallas traded star running back Herschel Walker to the Minnesota Vikings in 1989 for eight draft picks. Johnson chose an undersized running back from the University of Florida named Emmitt Smith as one of these first picks.

Smith was the latest piece of the puzzle for Johnson. The Cowboys had picked quarterback Troy Aikman and receiver Michael Irvin in the first round of the previous two drafts. All three players became known as the "Big Three" and won three Super Bowls with the Cowboys in the early 1990s. Their best season came in 1992, and it was the offense that brought the Cowboys most of the attention. Six players, including Smith, made the Pro Bowl. Smith had an NFL-best 1,713 yards and scored an NFL-best 18 touchdowns in 1992. When he retired in 2004, Smith became the NFL's all-time leading rusher with over 18,000 yards.

Dallas Cowboys players Emmitt Smith and Michael Ervin celebrate their victory over the Buffalo Bills in Super Bowl XXVII.

Troy Aikman wasn't bad either, throwing for 3,445 yards (1,396 to Irvin) and 23 touchdowns. With an average player age of 26, the young Cowboys finished 13–3 and qualified for the playoffs for the second time in Johnson's fourth season. It was the San Francisco 49ers who went 14–2 and had home-field advantage in the playoffs. That didn't bother the Cowboys, though. They went into San Francisco's Candlestick Park and beat the Niners 30–20 in the NFC championship game. After winning such an intense road game, the Cowboys were confident going into Super Bowl XXVII, where they faced the Buffalo Bills.

HISTORY BOX

Lonesome Losers

The Buffalo Bills did something no other team in the NFL has ever done—they played in four straight Super Bowls from 1991 to 1994 and lost all four of them. In Super Bowl XXV, the team lost on a last-second field goal to the New York Giants. But the Buffalo Bills produced many great players and a great coach, too. Coach Marv Levy and quarterback Jim Kelly have been inducted into the Pro Football Hall of Fame and running back Thurman Thomas and defensive end Bruce Smith are likely to be inducted in the future.

1992 Dallas Cowboys

Pro Bowlers:

Troy Aikman	(QB)	Jay Novacek	(TE)
Michael Irvin	(WR)	Emmitt Smith	(RB)
Nate Newton	(OL)	Mark Stepnoski	(OL)

Head coach: Jimmy Johnson

1992 Dallas Cowboys

The Buffalo Bills were in the Super Bowl for the third straight year, but had lost the previous two years. The Cowboys handed the Bills their third loss, beating them 52–17. Aikman was the MVP, throwing for four touchdowns. The real star was the Dallas' defense, causing a record 9 **turnovers** and scoring 35 points off of Buffalo mistakes. The Cowboys went on to win the next Super Bowl and won it again two years later, without Coach Johnson. The Cowboys became the first team to win the Super Bowl three times in a four-year span.

Troy Aikman helped the Cowboys win the 1992 Super Bowl.

HISTORY BOX

Salary Cap Era

The Cowboys were football's first **dynasty** to have a salary cap. A salary cap is a set amount of money that each team can spend on player salaries in one season. For example, in 2005, the cap was $80 million. No team could spend more than that amount on its players. The first season the cap was in place was 1994. That meant the Cowboys couldn't afford to keep all of their players. If they did, their total salary figure would be over the cap limit. Instead of being able to keep most of the players on the roster, the Cowboys had to let some of their players have **free agency**, and this broke up the team.

1992 Record

Won	Lost
16	3

NFC Divisional Playoff
Beat Philadelphia Eagles 34–10

NFC Championship Game
Beat San Francisco 49ers 30–20

Super Bowl
Beat Buffalo Bills 52–17

Games played

Week	Vs	Result	Score
1	Washington Redskins	W	23–10
2	at New York Giants	W	34–28
3	Phoenix Cardinals	W	31–20
4	BYE WEEK		
5	at Philadelphia Eagles	L	7–31
6	Seattle Seahawks	W	27–0
7	Kansas City Chiefs	W	17–10
8	at Los Angeles Raiders	W	28–13
9	Philadelphia Eagles	W	20–10
10	at Detroit Lions	W	37–3
11	Los Angeles Rams	L	23–27
12	at Phoenix Cardinals	W	16–10
13	New York Giants	W	30–3
14	at Denver Broncos	W	31–27
15	at Washington Redskins	L	17–20
16	at Atlanta Falcons	W	41–17
17	Chicago Bears	W	21–14

The Cowboys lost just 3 games in the 1992 season.

1998 Denver Broncos

When the Denver Broncos started the 1998 season 13–0, a perfect season seemed possible. With a Super Bowl title from the previous season under their belts, the Broncos played with confidence and talent. However, the Broncos lost twice before the regular-season ended. They were still a great team, with two of the best players in the game and Coach Mike Shanahan. Quarterback John Elway and running back Terrell Davis were two great football players who made their mark in history.

Nearing the end of his career, 38-year-old John Elway no longer played like he did when he was younger. Davis made up for this. Davis had one of the best seasons in NFL history with 2,008 rushing yards in 1998. He also added 23 touchdowns.

Terrell Davis scored many important touchdowns for the Broncos.

John Elway (1960–   )

You can't miss John Elway's name in the NFL record books. He won more games (148) than any other quarterback in NFL history. He also led more fourth-quarter comebacks (47) than anyone else. He made the Pro Bowl nine times, won the NFL MVP once, and won the Super Bowl MVP once. Is it any wonder Elway is thought by many to be football's best quarterback ever?

With eight Pro Bowl players, the Broncos had 501 points on offense. If Davis wasn't running, Elway was throwing to tight end Shannon Sharpe or receiver Rod Smith. After the Broncos had a 13–0 start to the season, the New York Giants upset them in Week 14. They also lost the next game to the Miami Dolphins and finished the season 14–2. This made fans wonder if they could repeat as Super Bowl champions. They provided the answer in the playoffs. In the divisional round, they beat the Dolphins. The Broncos went on to the AFC Championship game and beat the New York Jets 23–10 to make it to Super Bowl XXXIII, where they faced the Atlanta Falcons.

1998 Denver Broncos

The Atlanta Falcons were no match for the Broncos. John Elway, playing in his last game, threw to Smith for an 80-yard touchdown pass. The Broncos never looked back. Davis, who had won the Super Bowl MVP the year before, rushed for 102 yards and a touchdown, but Elway was the real star. He passed for 336 yards and 1 touchdown and ran for another in the Broncos 34–19 win. Elway, who was named the game's MVP, retired four months later. This made him the only quarterback to retire as a Super Bowl champion.

HISTORY BOX

The Dream Game That Never Happened

During the 1998 season, the Denver Broncos cruised through the AFC with a 14–2 record. In most years, that would be the best in the NFL. Over in the NFC, the Minnesota Vikings put together the highest-scoring season in NFL history. They had 556 points in 16 games, and went a nearly perfect 15–1 behind quarterback Randall Cunningham and receiver Randy Moss. The Vikings won their playoff opener 41–21 over the Arizona Cardinals to reach the NFC championship game. But the Vikings never got to play the Broncos in that Super Bowl. They lost at home, in overtime, to an Atlanta Falcons' team that had a 14–2 record that season.

1998 Denver Broncos

Pro Bowlers:

Steve Atwater	(DB)	Ed McCaffrey	(WR)
Terrell Davis	(RB)	Tom Nalen	(OL)
John Elway	(QB)	Bill Romanowski	(LB)
Tony Jones	(OL)	Shannon Sharpe	(TE)

Head coach: Mike Shanahan

1998 Record

Won	Lost	AFC Divisional Playoff
17	2	Beat Miami Dolphins 38–3

AFC Championship Game
Beat New York Jets 23–10

Super Bowl
Beat Atlanta Falcons 34–19

Games played

Week	Vs	Result	Score
1	New England Patriots	W	27–21
2	Dallas Cowboys	W	42–23
3	at Oakland Raiders	W	34–17
4	at Washington Redskins	W	38–16
5	Philadelphia Eagles	W	41–16
6	at Seattle Seahawks	W	21–16
7	BYE WEEK		
8	Jacksonville Jaguars	W	37–24
9	at Cincinnati Bengals	W	33–26
10	San Diego Chargers	W	27–10
11	at Kansas City Chiefs	W	30–7
12	Oakland Raiders	W	40–14
13	at San Diego Chargers	W	31–16
14	Kansas City Chiefs	W	35–31
15	at New York Giants	L	16–20
16	at Miami Dolphins	L	21–31
17	Seattle Seahawks	W	28–21

The Broncos celebrate yet another touchdown.

1999 St. Louis Rams

In 1998, the St. Louis Rams won four games and lost twelve. Going into the final season of the 1990s, the Rams had the worst combined record in the NFC for the decade's first nine seasons. That all changed in 1999, when the Rams became NFL champions for the first time in the franchise's history.

After a 4–12 season, the Rams decided to improve their offense. In the off-season, they traded with the Indianapolis Colts for running back Marshall Faulk. The Rams also signed Trent Green, a free-agent quarterback from the Washington Redskins, to continue making a great offense. Green was a career backup quarterback with Washington before he became a starter in 1998, due to injuries to the Redskins' starting quarterbacks. Dick Vermeil, the Rams' coach, liked Green and thought that he could be the quarterback to turn the Rams' luck around.

Marshall Faulk signed for the Rams before the start of the 1999 season.

Football in Los Angeles

As the second biggest city in the United States, Los Angeles has a natural fan base for pro football. The city had two pro teams, the Raiders and Rams, from 1982 to 1994. The Rams began playing in Los Angeles as far back as 1946. But since the 1994 season, the city, which has the Dodgers of Major League Baseball and two NBA franchises, the Lakers and the Clippers, has been without an NFL team.

The Rams selected receiver Torry Holt as their final pick in the draft. Holt starred at N.C. State University and had the speed and attitude Vermeil thought he needed to be a winner. As well as Holt, the Rams had receivers Isaac Bruce and Ricky Proehl and drafted another rookie receiver, Az-Zahir Hakim. The receivers, combined with Faulk catching passes out of the backfield, gave the Rams the fastest offense in the NFL. This offense became known as "The Greatest Show on Turf," a nickname indicating that the Rams played their home games on the artificial surface, turf.

Everything seemed in place until a major injury nearly ruined the Rams' 1999 season. In the team's first preseason game, Trent Green injured his knee and was lost for the entire season. Vermeil began the year by crying at the press conference to announce Green's injury. He would end the year crying, but for a different reason. The Rams had devoted their offense to Green and had no backup quarterback on the roster with NFL experience. Vermeil turned to Kurt Warner, an unknown backup quarterback, to replace Green.

1999 St. Louis Rams

Pro Bowlers:

Isaac Bruce	(WR)	Todd Lyght	(DB)
Kevin Carter	(DL)	Orlando Pace	(OL)
Marshall Faulk	(RB)	Kurt Warner	(QB)

Head coach: Dick Vermeil

1999 St. Louis Rams

Kurt Warner, who had been cut earlier in his career by the Green Bay Packers, had been playing professionally in Europe and in the indoor leagues. In fact, just two years earlier, Warner had been working in a grocery store in Iowa! To the surprise of the team, Kurt Warner was about to have one of the best seasons by an NFL quarterback ever. Warner was a perfect fit for the team's high-speed offense. With Warner leading the NFL with 41 touchdown passes, the Rams scored an NFL-best 526 points. Holt and Bruce combined to catch 129 passes and 18 touchdowns. Faulk was just as good, both catching the ball and running. He caught a team-high 87 passes for 1,048 yards. He also rushed for 1,381 yards. The Rams went from 4–12 in 1998 to 13–3 in 1999 and had the best record in the NFC.

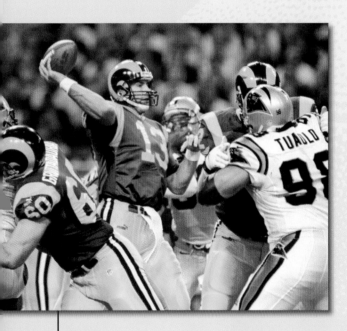

With home-field advantage in the playoffs, the Rams won two very different playoff games. They outscored the Minnesota Vikings 49–37 in the divisional round and then beat the Tampa Bay Buccaneers 11–6 in the NFC championship game. The Rams' defense came up big in the NFC Championship game, intercepting Tampa Bay quarterback Shaun King in the final moments to seal the victory and a trip to the Super Bowl.

Rams' quarterback Kurt Warner passes in a game against the Carolina Panthers.

The Rams used both their high-powered offense and their defense in Super Bowl XXXIV against the Tennessee Titans. Warner and Bruce hooked up on a 73-yard touchdown pass late in the fourth quarter to put the Rams ahead 23–16. Then the defense made the biggest stop of the season. The Titans drove within 10 yards of the tying touchdown in the final seconds. In the game's final play, Tennessee quarterback Steve McNair connected with receiver Kevin Dyson.

The Rams celebrate another victory in 1999.

But Rams' linebacker Mike Jones tackled Dyson 1-yard short of the end zone and the clock ran out. For the game, Warner set a Super Bowl record with 414 passing yards and was named the MVP as the Rams won their first Super Bowl. Coach Vermeil ended the championship season crying—tears of joy!

1999 Record

Won	Lost	NFC Divisional Playoff
16	3	Beat Minnesota Vikings 49–37

NFC Championship Game	Super Bowl
Beat Tampa Bay Buccaneers 11–6	Beat Tennessee Titans 23–16

Games played

Week	Vs	Result	Score
1	Baltimore Ravens	W	27–10
2	BYE WEEK		
3	Atlanta Falcons	W	35–7
4	at Cincinnati Bengals	W	38–10
5	San Francisco 49ers	W	42–20
6	at Atlanta Falcons	W	41–13
7	Cleveland Browns	W	34–3
8	at Tennessee Titans	L	21–24
9	at Detroit Lions	L	27–31
10	Carolina Panthers	W	35–10
11	at San Francisco 49ers	W	23–7
12	New Orleans Saints	W	43–12
13	at Carolina Panthers	W	34–21
14	at New Orleans Saints	W	30–14
15	New York Giants	W	31–10
16	Chicago Bears	W	34–12
17	at Philadelphia Eagles	L	31–38

After winning fifteen straight games and ending the 2003 season with one of the most thrilling Super Bowl wins ever, the New England Patriots got even better! As hard as it is to top a championship season, that's exactly what the Patriots did in 2004.

After winning Super Bowl XXXVIII on a last-second field goal by Adam Vinatieri, Patriots' coach Bill Belichick did not sit back and celebrate. He worked even harder. The key to the Patriots' first two Super Bowl titles rested on a great defense and the arm of quarterback Tom Brady. But before the 2004 season, the Patriots added running back Corey Dillon in a trade with the Cincinnati Bengals. The Patriots went 14–2 in 2004 and extended their NFL-record winning streak to 21 games. It was the first loss of the season, on Halloween at Pittsburgh, that showed how valuable Dillon was to the team.

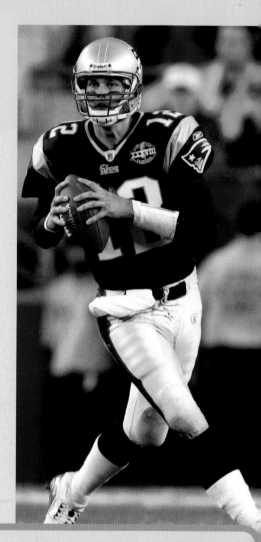

Tom Brady (1977–   )

Incredibly, Tom Brady was the 199th pick in the 2000 NFL draft. What the NFL scouts couldn't see in Brady was his ability to lead in the game's tightest moments. But Brady's natural talent and calmness eventually won fans and coaches over. He especially showed this in 2001, when he subbed for injured starter Drew Bledsoe. With just 3 career pass attempts to his credit, Brady led his team to an 11–3 finish and to the Super Bowl. In Super Bowl XXXVI, Brady led the Patriots to a 20–17 victory and won MVP honors. Two years later he repeated the Super Bowl title and MVP double. After leading the Patriots to a third Super Bowl title in 2004, Brady had a perfect 9–0 record in the playoffs. This was not bad for the 199th pick!

The Pittsburgh Steelers scored the game's first 21 points and went on to defeat the Patriots 34–20. It was the Patriots' first loss of the 2004 season and first since the beginning of the 2003 season. Dillon did not play against the Steelers because of a leg injury. Without Dillon, who finished the season with 1,635 yards, Brady spent the entire game trying to throw against a tough Steelers' defense.

Adam Vinatieri kicks the game-winning field goal in Super Bowl XXXVIII.

2004 New England Patriots

The Patriots got another chance against Pittsburgh. This time, Dillon was healthy and this time a trip to the Super Bowl was on the line. In the AFC championship game, the Patriots returned to Pittsburgh's Heinz Field and left no doubt about who was the AFC's best team. Despite the better record, at 14–0, Pittsburgh couldn't stop the Patriots or Dillon. He rushed for 73 yards and a touchdown to help crush the Steelers 41–27 and take the Patriots on to the Super Bowl.

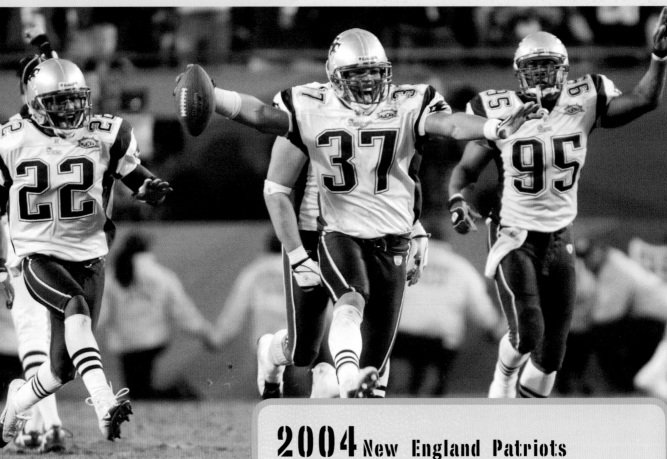

The New England Patriots celebrate after an interception in Super Bowl XXXIX against the Philadelphia Eagles.

2004 New England Patriots

Pro Bowlers:

Adam Vinatieri	(K)	Richard Seymour	(DL)
Tom Brady	(QB)	Tedy Bruschi	(LB)
Corey Dillon	(RB)		

Head coach: Bill Belichik

K=Kicker

2004 Record

Won	Lost
17	2

AFC Championship Game
Beat Pittsburgh Steelers 41–27

AFC Divisional Playoff
Beat Indianapolis Colts 20–3

Super Bowl
Beat Philadelphia Eagles 24–21

Games played

Week	Vs	Result	Score
1	Indianapolis Colts	W	27–24
2	at Arizona Cardinals	W	23–12
3	BYE WEEK		
4	at Buffalo Bills	W	31–17
5	Miami Dolphins	W	24–10
6	Seattle Seahawks	W	30–20
7	New York Jets	W	13–7
8	at Pittsburgh Steelers	L	20–34
9	at St. Louis Rams	W	40–22
10	Buffalo Bills	W	29–6
11	at Kansas City Chiefs	W	27–19
12	Baltimore Ravens	W	24–3
13	at Cleveland Browns	W	42–15
14	Cincinnati Bengals	W	35–28
15	at Miami Dolphins	L	28–29
16	at New York Jets	W	23–7
17	San Francisco 49ers	W	21–7

The Patriots faced the Eagles in the Super Bowl. The Eagles were the team with the best record from the NFC. The Patriots got their usual outstanding effort from their defense, especially linebacker Tedy Bruschi and safety Rodney Harrison. Dillon was solid again, with 75 yards on 18 carries and 1 touchdown. The Patriots won Super Bowl XXXIX by three points. This win put the 2004 Patriots among the sport's greatest teams.

HISTORY BOX

From Losers to Winners

Before Bill Belichick took the Patriots to three Super Bowl titles, the Patriots had a history of losing. Even when the Patriots were good, they always lost the big games. All of this changed in the 2001 season. Belichick and quarterback Tom Brady led the Patriots to a victory over the St. Louis Rams in Super Bowl XXXVI. The Patriots went on to win the Super Bowl twice in the next three years to change their reputation for losing.

The Final Score

There's no arguing football's popularity in this country or its place in sports. The argument in football is who the best team to ever play the game was. The sport has grown with each decade, not only in popularity, but also with the speed and size of its players. Many people might ask, could the players on the 1950 Cleveland Browns or even the 1962 Green Bay Packers compete with the bigger players of today's generation?

Pro football has a long history, with talented players and the determined coaches that led them to championships. Each decade in the NFL can be broken down by which team really stood out. The Packers ruled pro football in the 1960s. The Pittsburgh Steelers took over in the 1970s and the San Francisco 49ers in the 1980s. The Dallas Cowboys took their turn in the 1990s and now the New England Patriots have established their greatness with their recent Super Bowl wins. Each year, different teams battle against one another for a chance to go to the Super Bowl. The pro football divisions have their own rivalries. With each draft pick, pro football keeps getting more exciting. One thing is certain in pro football: the game will only get better!

Pro football always attracts big crowds.

Timeline

1922: The American Professional Football Association changes its name to the National Football League (NFL), the same organization that rules the sport today.

1936: The first NFL draft takes place.

1943: The NFL makes all players wear helmets.

1950: Cleveland Browns beat Los Angeles Rams 30–28 in the NFL championship game.

1962: Green Bay Packers defeat New York Giants 16–7 in the NFL championship game.

1966: The NFL and AFL combine to form a 24-team league and agree to play the NFL-AFL championship game, which later becomes known as the Super Bowl.

1968: Paul Brown helps create the Cincinnati Bengals, an expansion team.

1970: "Monday Night Football" debuts on ABC.

1973: 1972 Miami Dolphins beat Washington Redskins 14–7 in the Super Bowl.

1976: 1975 Pittsburgh Steelers beat Dallas Cowboys 21–17 in the Super Bowl.

1978: The NFL schedule changes from fourteen games to sixteen games during the regular season.

1986: 1985 Chicago Bears beat New England Patriots 46–10 in the Super Bowl.

1990: 1989 San Francisco 49ers beat Denver Broncos 55–10 in the Super Bowl.

1993: 1992 Dallas Cowboys beat Buffalo Bills 52–17 in the Super Bowl.

1994: NFL salary cap is put into place.

1999: 1998 Denver Broncos beat Atlanta Falcons 34–19 in the Super Bowl.

2000: 1999 St. Louis Rams beat Tennessee Titans 23–16 in the Super Bowl.

2002: The Houston Texans join the league as an expansion team, bringing the NFL to its current total of 32 franchises.

2005: 2004 New England Patriots defeat Philadelphia Eagles 24–21 in the Super Bowl.

Glossary

blitz when the defensive team rushes the quarterback as soon as the ball is snapped back

center offensive player who hikes the ball to the quarterback

conference in pro football, teams are grouped into two conferences—American Football Conference and National Football Conference

cornerback defensive player who usually covers a wide receiver

decade period of ten years

defensive end defensive player who rushes the quarterback

defensive tackle defensive player who lines up on the inside of a defensive line

dominant leader. A dominant team is one that seems unbeatable.

draft selection process for professional sports teams

dynasty in sports, a team that maintains its great position for a long time

end zone area between the end line and the goal line; where a team tries to score touchdowns

franchise professional sports team organization. For example, the Chicago Bears are a franchise.

free agency when a player's contract with a team expires, and he is then free to sign a new contract with another team.

fullback offensive player who blocks for the halfback and quarterback

inconsistent only playing well some of the time

linebacker defender positioned directly behind the defensive lineman

lineman defensive or offensive player positioned directly on the line of scrimmage

Most Valuable Player (MVP) award given each year to the best player in the league, or the best player from the Super Bowl

National Football League (NFL) major professional football league in the United States

overtime extra playing periods added to the game when it ends in a tie.

Pro Bowl an all-star game in football that features the best players in both conferences

Pro Football Hall of Fame organization that honors the best footbal players and coaches throughout history

quarterback player who takes the snap from the center and runs the offense

receiver offensive player who catches the football

running back player that is positioned right behind the center once he receives the snap

rushing when the defensive team tries to get past blockers and sack the quarterback

safety defensive player who helps the cornerbacks

shutouts game in which one team fails to score

Super Bowl championship game of the NFL

tight end sixth offensive lineman who is also a pass receiver. In the early days of football, all receivers were "ends," which is equal to the modern-day tight end.

turnover when a team with possession of the ball accidentally loses it

underdog not expected to win

wide receiver offensive player who catches passes from the quarterback

yard unit of measurement on the football field. The playing field is 100 yards in length.

Further Information

Further reading

Buckley, Jr., James. *Football*. New York:
Dorling Kindersley Publishing Inc., 2000

Nichols, John. *Chicago Bears*. Mankato, MN:
The Creative Company, 2000

Owens, Thomas S. *Football Stadiums*. Minneapolis:
Twenty-First Century Books, Inc., 2004

Roensch, Greg. *Vince Lombardi*. New York:
The Rosen Publishing Group, Inc., 2003

Stewart, Mark Alan. *Tom Brady*: *Heart of the Huddle*.
Minneapolis: Twenty-First Century Books, Inc., 2004

Stewart, Mark. *Terrell Davis*: *Toughing It Out*.
Minneapolis: Twenty-First Century Books, Inc., 2004

Tuttle, Dennis R. *Football*. Langhorne, PA:
Chelsea House Publishers, 1999

Addresses

Pro Football Hall of Fame
2121 George Halas Drive NW
Canton, Ohio 44708
www.profootballhof.com

The National Football League (NFL)
www.nfl.com

All the Internet addresses (URLs) given in this book were valid at the time of going to press.
However, due to the dynamic nature of the Internet, some addresses may have changed, or sites
may have changed or ceased to exist since publication. While the author and publishers regret any
inconvenience this may cause readers, no responsibility for any such changes can be accepted by
either the author or the publishers.

The Final Score